Touch Ten Souls in Ten Minutes

Ten-minute sketches invoking spiritural
growth in youth ministry

YOUTH EDITION

APRIL BASKIN

WestBow
PRESS
A DIVISION OF THOMAS NELSON

WestBow Press books may be ordered through booksellers or by contacting:

WestBow Press
A Division of Thomas Nelson
1663 Liberty Drive
Bloomington, IN 47403
www.westbowpress.com
1-(866) 928-1240

Because of the dynamic nature of the Internet, any web addresses or links contained in this book may have changed since publication and may no longer be valid. The views expressed in this work are solely those of the author and do not necessarily reflect the views of the publisher, and the publisher hereby disclaims any responsibility for them.

Any people depicted in stock imagery provided by Thinkstock are models, and such images are being used for illustrative purposes only.

Certain stock imagery © Thinkstock.

ISBN: 978-1-4497-4203-4 (sc)

Library of Congress Control Number: 2012904170

Printed in the United States of America

WestBow Press rev. date: 03/19/2012

I write this book in memory of Eugene H. Jacobs.
Granddaddy taught me church first, everything else second.

I dedicate this book to you, the reader.
May God continue to give you a desire to multiply His holy kingdom.

ACKNOWLEDGMENTS

This book would not be possible without the family, friends and saints of God who nurtured me as I wrestled with finding a purpose for my talents in God's kingdom. I first want to thank my Lord and Savior Jesus Christ. You are Potter, Father, and Friend to me. Even when I walked away, you stayed at my side. Nothing compares to you. Thank-you to my husband Branden Baskin for loving me and constantly encouraging me to "write out my goals" you make my dreams possible. Thank-you Joie Jean for making motherhood everything I dreamed it would be; I see the world differently because of you. Thank-you mom and dad, Brian and Lisa Watson for sitting back, observing each of your children individually and molding us as needed. I would not know what to do with all the abstract thoughts compiled in my mind had you not told me I am an artist. Thank-you grandma Jovanna Jacobs, you are a wise woman with a selfless giving heart. I strive to be like you daily. Thanks to all my siblings for years of laughter and tons of writing material. Thank-you Maxwell and Cory McCants, you were my very first cast members ever. Thank-you Sharon Turner and Nina Schultz for your shoulders, which are full of my tears from years past. I appreciate your friendship and sisterhood. I owe so much to Mark and Maureen Mascellino for your patience, Godly example, instruction and outstanding sense of humor. Thank-you Bishop and Sister David Robinson, and Bishop and Sister Scotty Teets for listening to Gods calling upon your life. So many lives will enter heaven due to your obedience to His will. Finally I want to thank my close brothers and sisters in Christ, Aiyana and Dirjon Waldron, Paul, Andrea, Nicole and Brandon McNeil, Lauren and Stephanie Miller, Craig and Shaina Henry, Stanley and Eileen Diih, Maurice Mullings, Felipe Rodriguez, and the host of saints who have relentlessly helped bring the plays in this book to life. Thank-you for giving and continuing to give to drama ministry. My life is forever changed through your sacrifice.

CONTENTS

PROLOGUE

Visual storytelling and performing arts is used in churches worldwide as a form of evangelism known as Drama Ministry. Think of a sermon that drastically affected your life. Reminisce on the very moment God enlightened your perspective of a particular situation simply using His word and an open vessel to minister it. Reflect on your emotional state prior to the sermon; savor the memory of God's unmatched love consoling you after the preaching. Your life was changed because the gospel was presented to you like never before. Each of the thoughts you just processed was followed by an image. What if you took this imagery a step further than psychological pictures? The books of the bible, the sermon of a well-known preacher or even your own testimonial walk with Christ can be transformed into a visual story unfolding God's unconditional grace. Through that story, someone's life could be drastically impacted same as you were in your memory. Not to fret, the story doesn't have to be adapted into a grand Broadway production to be deemed a success. Stage plays containing biblical principles and sound doctrine can fascinate an audience as quick as ten minutes!

My two-year-old daughter has a collection of children's books. I try to make an effort to read with her in the evenings. One night, while cleaning our home, I overheard her actually reading one of our favorite stories on her own. With a great deal of excitement I ran to her room, overjoyed that my toddler was a miracle genius. She could read at age two. I sat down beside her and asked her to start the book from the beginning. She also gleamed with joy, as mommy was noticeably proud of her. My daughter began to read again and completed the book effortlessly. Delighted in her achievement, I pulled another book from the shelf and asked her to read. She confidently opened the book and cleared her throat. She read, "the boy rides a doggy". This was not the first sentence of the story. However, there was a picture clear as day, of a boy riding a doggy. I laughed realizing the secret to my daughter's previous success. Visuals have a way of helping children remember the story a little better. Visual stories or drama presentations with themes and plotlines based on biblical principles is an imaginative method used for understanding and applying the gospel to our lives. It is my experience that ministry by way of dramatic production has the ability to engage, educate and entertain our churches and the communities in which we function. Play productions are awesome fundraisers, outreach tools, and offer a platform for members of the church (young people in particular) to fellowship while learning the value of ministry. This collection of short plays will allow you to tap into an innovative ministry sure to captivate young souls in search of Christ.

The task of the director or drama team leader is a grand responsibility, and at times very exhausting. Finding a committed cast, planning rehearsals, purchasing props and costumes, the list goes on. Over the last ten years, I have made several mistakes and learned many lessons. I quickly learned the first priority of a drama team leader is prayer. God needs to be involved in every facet of ministry, including the arts. He is truly the most skillful artist we will ever know.

Majoring in theatre arts in college and touring as a professional actor laid the foundation for my position as a director. Several drama ministry books have helped me understand the fundamentals of building a successful drama team. Through reading them, I have developed a clear understanding of leadership in arts ministry. However, when a dedicated cast as come forward, and all the designers, seamstress, and stagehands are in place . . . what is the script about?

The script is an essential part of drama ministry commonly overlooked. At times, our scripts are non-thought-out ideas or scattered thoughts from a brainstorming session with others. We get so very excited to find the perfect actors, fabulous costumes and eye-catching scenery that we neglect to put effort into the script. In drama ministry, the imagery in a play should help your audience remember the story. Therefore, story must be thought provoking, cohesive and most importantly minster God's truth. I have witnessed so many church plays with outstanding production elements but very little message of the gospel. We often feel safe reenacting biblical stories but seldom help our audience connect the story to their life. In these cases, are we ministering or entertaining? A drama team has the exciting job of doing what any pastor or evangelist does from a pulpit, however we get to make it sparkle. We add lights, backdrops, funny characters and sound effects. Still, it is important for us to have a clear message and a well-organized story to effectively minister. We need to touch the hearts of our audience. This book is designed for the drama team that is ready to see lives changed through their performance. *Touch Ten Souls in Ten Minutes* is a collection of short contemporary plays full of scripture and entertaining plotlines. The sketches emphasize topics such as *Backsliding, Body Image, Bullying, Drug Abuse, Gossip, Music, Modesty, Peer Pressure, Prayer* and many more. A simple ten-minute play has the power to touch the hearts of ten young souls and change their walk in Christ forever.

STRANGERS IN THE WORLD

Cast: 2 males, 2 females, 2 News Reporters, 1 Corrections Officer, 1 Judge male or female.

A brief moment of silence has transformed into an apprehensive hush settled within a scarce number of homes throughout the nation. The few citizens who still declare themselves Christians, hold secret prayer meetings in their basements, pleading for God to rescue the Martyr Four. The year is 2020. The world suffers from a severe case of stagflation. The United States particularly is overflowing with regions submerged in hazardous living because of the early 21st century economic collapse. Over the past three years, several countries' desperate attempt to redevelop their homelands has ended in numerous world wars. To put an end to warfare, as of January 1st 2020, the newly implemented Centralized Government Division of the United Nations passed the Common god Law, the purpose being to unify the world in peace through one universal religion for all. This is the tale of those who refused to conform.

Themes: End Time, Rapture of the church.

Related Scriptures: Psalms 55:22, Philippians 2:14, Deuteronomy 31:6, Revelation 13:7

"Strangers in the World" New York Metro Holiday Youth Convention 2011
Photographer: David A. Bertram
Graphic: Rite Track Design

The action of the play takes place in a prison cell. There is darkness. We hear the SOUND of exhaustion, heavy breathing, and fear coming from four timid teenagers locked in a PRISON CELL. We SEE—rapid movement of light, which comes from the inmates FLASHLIGHTS. The four teenagers whisper various scriptures. Stage left, sits an aggravated CORRECTIONS OFFICER. He reads a MAGAZINE, and tries his best to ignore the teenage inmates.

MILES

Ye shall hear of wars and rumors of wars for nation shall rise against nation, and kingdom against kingdom: And there shall be famines, and pestilences, and earthquakes, in divers places. All these are the beginning of sorrows.

OFFICER

Pipe down.

EMILY

Nation shall rise against nation, and kingdom against kingdom: And great earthquakes shall be in divers places, and famines, and pestilences; and fearful sights and great signs shall there be from heaven.

OFFICER

Did you here me?

KEKE

Men shall be lovers of their own selves, covetous, boasters, proud, blasphemers, disobedient to parents, unthankful, unholy,

OFFICER

I said quiet.

JESSICA

Without natural affection, trucebreakers,
false accusers, incontinent, fierce,
Despisers of those that are good, Traitors,
heady, high-minded,

OFFICER

Don't make me open this cell.

MILES

Lovers of pleasures more than lovers of
God; having a form of godliness, but
denying the power thereof

OFFICER

Enough!

ALL INMATES

(yelling)

Then shall they deliver you up to be
afflicted, and shall kill you: and ye shall
be hated of all nations for my name's sake

(they all begin loud praise and worship)

Lights rise to full

OFFICER

(annoyed)

Regardless of how the judge decides to
sentence you kids, I'll get the warden to
give you a month solitary confinement if
you don't pipe down. All of you!

(looking toward the audience)

Well look there, breaking news. See that
kids? They talking about you guys on TV.

Hope you and every other Christian like you gets what you deserve.

MILES

We trust in our Lord Jesus. There is nothing that you, or the judge can say that will change that.

OFFICER

Pipe down, I'm watching the news.

The SOUND of a "breaking news flash" Enter REPORTER 1

REPORTER 1

Today marks the conclusion of the litigation between the International Criminal Court and the religious group dubbed The Martyr Four. Martyr meaning a person who endures suffering because of their beliefs, And of course the "Four" represents the four high school students who were caught praying to Jesus in their school cafeteria six months ago.

Enter REPORTER 2

REPORTER 2

The intensity in the air is thick. The world waits to hear the judge's decision. Years ago, the Centralized Government Division of the United Nations decided there is only one way to bring world peace.

REPORTER 1

Put an end to religious differences; unite the world under one religion for all. The first amendment to the US constitution was ceased.

REPORTER 2

Everyone in the world was ordered to believe in the Common god Law.

REPORTER 1

It is against the law to believe in anything other than the Common god. Will the Martyr Four spend the rest of their lives in prison? Or be sentenced to death by lethal injection?

REPORTER 2

There are more than likely thousands of people all over the world, who still claim to be a Christian. Holding secret prayer meetings in their basements. Let these kids, the Martyr Four be an example to you.

REPORTER 1

There is no right or wrong in this situation, there is the law, and there is breaking the law. Praising and praying to Jesus is against the law.

KEKE

How much longer before the judge makes her decision?

MILES

Don't focus on that Keke. Focus on prayer.

EMILY

Prayer? Miles prayer has got us nowhere!

JESSICA

Don't talk like that it scares me.

MILES

Fear is not of God.

EMILY

It's an emotion, an emotion we all are feeling.

EMILY

(to Miles)

This is all your fault.

KEKE

Don't start arguing you guys.

EMILY

Mom and dad warned him he was too bold with his Christianity. He was the one who made us pray that day in the cafeteria.

MILES

How can you talk about me like that, I'm your blood.

EMILY

You're the reason I'm going to die.

JESSICA

We are not going to die. All we did was say grace before we ate our lunch. It's only a matter of time before we are free. Hey maybe God will bless us, and that judge will get the chicken pox AND swine flu! She will be too sick to sentence us!

KEKE

Yes Lord, work a miracle.

MILES

You are already free. You are free indeed. We were set free when Christ died at Calvary.

EMILY

Are the bars on this prison cell is freedom? What about these handcuffs? Are they freedom?

KEKE

These handcuffs are the beginning of our testimony.

MILES

Amen Keke.

EMILY

Oh please.

MILES

I know its hard little sister. But you have to hold on to your faith. It's been a rough journey.

EMILY

Its been six months

MILES

The road ahead may be tougher.

EMILY

It's been six months.

JESSICA

But this too shall pass.

EMILY

It has been six months. I thought all this stuff was supposed to happen during the time of tribulation. I thought God was going to rapture the church!

KEKE

He will. The bible tells us this world will wax worse and worse as the rapture of the church nears.

EMILY

This is beyond worse. I may die because I'm a Christian.

MILES

This is nothing new Emily. Because we are American, we are removed from persecution? No way. People have been killed for loving Christ for years. We always think it's supposed to happen in some third world country.

EMILY

Where is the rapture?

MILES

It's coming.

EMILY

I don't believe that anymore. Even our own parents have conformed to the Common god Law.

MILES

On Christ the solid rock I stand.

Enter REPORTER 1 and 2

REPORTER 1

We now have the Honorable Susan Vanderbelt outside the United Nations court ready with her decision.

Enter JUDGE, she is a stern woman, on a mission.

REPORTER 2

Judge Vanderbelt, the world waits for your judgment.

JUDGE VANDERBELT

After hearing both sides. I considered the argument of the defense. the Declaration of Independence and the Prayer Proclamation of 1789 hint The United States was built on a Christian foundation. To punish individuals who still practice those beliefs would be unconstitutional. However, the previous laws of the land will not supersede the current laws of the land. The Martyr Four are only teenagers, but they will someday be adults. Then, they will have the ability to convince others to conform to Christianity. Therefore, on behalf of the International Court System I motion all parties dubbed as the Martyr Four a threat to humanity. They are sentenced to death by lethal injection. Court dismissed.

ALL INMATES cry with agony.

MILES

Let us pray.

EMILY

Miles, I can't do this.

JESSICA

Please Emily.

EMILY

No. Ever since I was a kid being a
Christian has kept me from having a life.
It has restricted my clothes, my friends,
my fun, and now it is costing me my life.
I want to be happy.

(to Officer)

Let me out. I am not a Christian.

OFFICER

You have come to your senses.

MILES

No, she is just hungry, bring her some
food please.

EMILY

I am not hungry; I want to see the judge.

KEKE

Do not do this Emily.

JESSICA

I have always looked up to you.

EMILY

Then come with me.

JESSICA

I can't.

EMILY

Why not?

JESSICA

I've come too far.

Enter Judge

JUDGE VANDERBELT

You wanted to see me.

EMILY

Yes your Honor. I am not a Christian. I
want world peace; I am a believer of the
Common god.

JUDGE VANDERBELT

And Jesus Christ. Who is he to you?

EMILY

Nothing, just a figment of my childhood
imagination.

JUDGE VANDERBELT

Release her.

The Officer removes Emily's handcuffs. She also gives him her inmate uniform. Emily
exits. Miles and the others weep for Emily.

JUDGE VANDERBELT

Don't weep for her, she came to her
senses.

Judge exit.

11

MILES

Keke, you remember when your
grandmother taught Sunday school.
Remember the song she made us sing
every single class.

No response.

MILES

You must remember it, we sang it
everyday for years.

KEKE

(in song)

"Jesus loves me this I know."

MILES

"for the bible tells me so"

KEKE MILES JESSICA

*"Little ones to Him belong. They are weak
but He is strong . . ."*

We Hear—the SOUND of an earthquake. BLACKOUT

Lights rise

Enter REPORTER 1

REPORTER 1

Strange events have taken place over the
world today. I number of people have
gone missing.

REPORTER 2

It is a disappearing act. One moment you
were standing next to someone, and then
in the blink of an eye, they were gone.

National government officials are not able
to explain it.

Suddenly, EMILY rushes through the audience.

EMILY

Let me in! Let me in!

OFFICER

How did you get in here! Don't you know
the world is in a state of emergency! Go
find safety!

EMILY

Please, please open the cell, I AM A
CHRISTIAN! This is the rapture. God
has returned for His faithful children.

OFFICER

You keep that crazy talk up and I'll lock
you up.

EMILY

I LOVE YOU JESUS!

The Officer puts Emily in handcuffs.

Lights rise in the prison cell. The cell is empty. The inmate uniforms are all that is left
of the remaining inmates.

OFFICER

Code 991! Code 991! The inmates are
missing too!

He hastily exits. Emily stands alone in the empty cell. Lights fade to black.

THE END

BAGGAGE CLAIM

Cast: 2 males, 2 females, 1 Pilot, 1 Flight Attendant male or female.

Baggage Claim is the story of a church youth group making their way to heaven discovering inheritance of God's kingdom requires letting go of worldly desires.

Themes: Strongholds, Temptation, Drug Abuse, Vanity, Dating, Hypocrites.

Related Scriptures: Matthew 26:41, Colossians 3:2.

"Baggage Claim" UPCI North American Youth Congress 2011
Photographer: David A. Bertram
See live footage of this sketch at www.youtube.com/writeouswordentertainment

WE HERE—the SOUND of DUST moving in the WIND, followed by a louder SOUND of an aircraft PROPELLER compressing. In darkness, LAUGHTER echoes from a small youth group entering Heaven Bound Airways. KENYA, a young diva dressed in a fabulous oversized hat, fashion label bag and sunglasses enters with, MACY a vibrant free spirit. Best friends COLLIN and GERALD follow them; GERALD is adventurous while COLLIN is a reserved intellectual. LIGHTS RISE.

MACY

(looking in astonishment)

Wow, I had NO idea the airline would be this beautiful.

KENYA

Just look at the decor of this place. Persian rugs and drapery?

COLLIN

How can you tell?

MACY

She has an expert's eye.

GERALD

I can't believe it! I'm really on my way to Heaven. I've been to tons of exotic places, white water rafting through the West Indies, sky diving in Paris. But through all of that, I've never been more excited about a trip than the one I'm going on now.

COLLIN

It is going to be a journey of a lifetime.

GERALD

Amen.

KENYA

(adjusting her clothing)

I'm on my way to see Jesus. I had to put
on the best of my Sunday's best.

COLLIN

Com'on guys, lets get together, take a
picture.

The group gathers.

COLLIN

Okay, everyone say "JOURNEY TO
JESUS"

ALL

JOURNEY TO JESUS!

MACY snaps a photo with her CAMERA.

GERALD

Let us see it.

KENYA

Yeah how do I look?

The group all smile at the image.

GERALD

(looking at the camera)

Look'at there. That's us, headed for
eternal life.

We hear the SOUND of the FLIGHT ATTENDANT'S voice over an intercom.

INTERCOM V.O.

Now boarding flight 007 to the United
Kingdom of Heaven . . . .

MACY

That's us!

GERALD

Wait nobody's checking any bags?

COLLIN

Nah, lets just take them with us.

Enter FLIGHT ATTENDANT, a vivacious woman with a cheerful smile.

FLIGHT ATTENDANT

Welcome passengers, now boarding seats
A1 thru A15.

MACY

Alright guys, lets hit it.

FLIGHT ATTENDANT

(checking tickets)

Oh! *(insert your church name)* Youth
Group. We've been expecting you.

KENYA

Really? You want to upgrade us to first
class?

FLIGHT ATTENDANT

Sorry, there are no class systems on
Heaven Bound Airways. We all get there
the same way.

Lights rise on four seats, separated into two's by an isle. The group files in and places their bags under their seats.

FLIGHT ATTENDANT

Ladies and gentlemen, welcome aboard Heaven Bound Airways flight with non-stop service to The United Kingdom of Heaven. Please turn your attention to the flight attendant nearest you for our safety demonstration. Please follow along with the safety card located in the seat pocket in front of you.

MACY

What do you think Jesus will say when he sees us?

KENYA

Nice suit.

GERALD

I've been expecting you.

COLLIN

I believe it goes a little something like "Well done thou good and faith full servant."

MACY

"thou hast been faithful over a few things,"

GERALD

"I will make thee ruler over many things"

KENYA

Enter into the joy of the Lord!

MACY

WE'RE GOING TO HEAVEN!

FLIGHT ATTENDANT

Also, make sure all carry-on items are stored in the overhead bins, or under the seat in front of you. There are emergency exits on this aircraft; In the front, in the back, and located over the wings.

GERALD

Would you say this is more of a animal crackers and juice box flight? Or Taco Bell and root beer float flight?

COLLIN

I've never heard of an airline giving out Taco Bell and Root Beer.

GERALD

Yeah, but this flight is going to Jesus' pad.

FLIGHT ATTENDANT

Remember, red lights mark and exit. In case there is a loss in cabin pressure, yellow oxygen masks will deploy from the ceiling compartment located above you. To secure, pull the mask towards you, secure the elastic strap to your head, and fasten it so it covers your mouth and nose. Breath normally.

KENYA

So, we get to heaven . . . get settled . . . what's the time frame like before Jesus starts handing out mansions?

MACY

I'm not really sure.

KENYA

Check these out.

She reveals a pair a SHINY GOLD platform HIGH HEELS.

MACY

What are those?

KENYA

Six inch, 10 karat, diamond incrusted heels. I want to accessorize with the streets of gold in Heaven.

MACY

Kenya, to us 10 karats is stunning but, we are going to HEAVEN. Our human minds cannot fantasize about our life there. When the bible talks about streets of gold, it is probably referring to a type of gold you or I cannot dream of.

KENYA

So, Jesus is going to think my shoes are tacky?

FLIGHT ATTENDANT

Please make sure your seat belt is fastened, you seat back and tray tables are in their full upright and lock position, and all carry on items are stored properly. Thank you for your attention, and we wish you a good flight on Heaven Bound Airways.

MACY

Hey guys, we are defiantly getting in to
heaven right?

KENYA

Well, sure . . . why wouldn't we?

GERALD

We always go to church.

COLLIN

We are saved according to the scriptures.
We pray, fast, and give our all to ministry.
That's all it takes. Don't worry guys. We
are going to Heaven.

Silence. The group engages in aircraft activities: reading magazines and listening to
music.

The SOUND of an ENGINE EXPLODES. The LIGHTS DIM.

MACY

What was that?

COLLIN

It's probably nothing, relax.

The Group TUMBLES LEFT.

KENYA

That is defiantly something!

COLLIN

Yeah, you are right. (he puts on his seat
belt) Gerald, go check it out.

GERALD

Huh? Why me? You are oldest.

COLLIN

You're the boldest. "Sky diving in Paris".

GERALD

(nervous)

Did I say sky diving? Oh, I meant sky
kite-ing, yeah, I flew a kite in Paris.

FLIGHT ATTENDANT

The captain has turned the seat belt safety
light on. Please, all passengers take your
seat and fasten your seat belts.

The group TUMBLES right. BLACKOUT. We hear SCREAMS of fear. Lights rise to dim.

MACY

I'm scared.

FLIGHT ATTENDANT

We are experiencing extreme turbulence.
I need all passengers to remain calm.

GERALD

What's happening?

Enter PILOT MATTHEWS, he is very shaken up.

PILOT MATTHEWS

Good evening ladies and gentleman, I am
Pilot Matthews.

GERALD

Nobody's flying the plane! We're going to die!

PILOT MATTHEWS

Please relax, I am the second pilot. I'm assisting the head pilot.

COLLIN

What's going on?

PILOT MATTHEWS

There is too much pressure on the aircraft, it's over loaded.

MACY

Don't tell me we have to jump out of this plane.

PILOT MATTHEWS

No, however it is imperative that we lighten the aircraft load. We need to disburse of some of the luggage on board.

KENYA

How?

PILOT MATTHEWS

Aircraft control has blocked all areas within a 50-mile radius of where we are flying. If we are going to release baggage, we must do it now. If we don't, there is no possible way we will make it to our final destination alive.

MACY

Kenya, give him your bag. It's the
heavyset.

COLLIN

It's true Kenya, you over packed.

KENYA

No way, I need my stuff.

The FLIGHT ATTENDANT grabs Kenya's bag. She REVEALS the opposite side of the
bag where the word VANITY is written in bold RED letters.

PILOT MATTHEWS

Hand it over, everyone take your seats.
The air pressure you will feel when I open
this door is immense.

KENYA

Wait! Take the others bags first.

FLIGHT ATTENDANT

Ma'am please take your seat.

KENYA

You don't understand, everything that
makes me who I am is in that bag!
Without it I feel worthless, ugly . . . I can't
go back to feeling that way.

GERALD

Kenya, we are talking about life and
death here.

KENYA

That stuff is important to me!

PILOT MATTHEWS

So important you're willing to die over it?

KENYA

I am a model Christian girl! I've been singing in the choir since I was six and directing it since I was nine. I started teaching Sunday school when I was twelve and teaching bible studies by sixteen. I'm on the ushers board, mission board, AND outreach board. YOU want to throw MY stuff off this airplane? I don't think so!

PILOT MATTHEWS

You are hindering your youth group's journey. Can't you see, the stuff that you are doing is great. However, that proud look on your face will be your death. If you do not let go of this bag, you will kill us all.

MACY

Please Kenya.

Kenya release the bag. Pilot Matthew Throws the SUIT CASE into the AUDIENCE.

FLIGHT ATTENDANT

Who is next?

MACY

Gerald has a big suite case like Kenya's.

GERALD

Hey! you keep talkin' about other folks bag? Where is your stuff?

FLIGHT ATTENDANT

Sir please.

GERALD

Honestly, it's not that heavy.

The lights flash, the group TUMBLES LEFT. The group screams with fear.

PILOT MATTHEWS

I need a bag.

KENYA

Give it up Gerald.

COLLIN, passes Gerald's bag, revealing to the audience the word HYPOCRITE written in bold RED letters.

GERALD

Wait; let me grab some things out of it.

PILOT MATTHEWS

It must go now.

GERALD

Please I'm begging you, half of my life is in that bag. Some of my friends, some of my music, places I like to go.

COLLIN

Who cares about stuff like that, we are on our way to eternal life.

GERALD

I care! I CAN'T BE a Christian all the time okay? I have to live, have fun. I have to experience the world.

MACY

I thought the whole point of this trip was
to leave the world behind.

GERALD

Don't you think I have tried to leave the
world behind? I like church, but I like
nightclubs too. I like getting drunk and
living life on the edge.

PILOT MATTHEWS

You have to make a decision now. Is it the
world or heaven?

COLLIN wrestles Gerald to the ground

COLLIN

Are you tying to kill us all?

GERALD

It is not about you guys, it's about me.

COLLIN

That is the problem!

Pilot Matthews throws Gerald's suitcase into the audience. The Flight Attendant
grabs MACY'S suitcase revealing the word ROMANTIC RELATIONSHIP in bold
red letters.

MACY

Hey! My bag is not that heavy.

FLIGHT ATTENDANT

All baggage must depart the aircraft.

MACY

No. Not mine.

KENYA

Yes Macy, we only have 50 miles to get rid
of this stuff.

MACY

What's the worst that can happen? Jesus,
will protect us. He will not let us die.

PILOT MATTHEWS

Refusing obedience is not Jesus letting
you die; it's you choosing to die. You
cannot pray the word away.

MACY

(desperate)

This bag is everything to me. I have put
so much into it. It's going to last forever.

FLIGHT ATTENDANT

Let it go.

MACY

I can't live with out it.

(to God)

I know sometime it causes me to
compromise your word, but please. Don't
make me get rid of it.

The BAG is tossed into the AUDIENCE. MACY weeps with KENYA.

KENYA

Collin, I only one left.

FLIGHT ATTENDANT

I didn't notice you boarded with a bag sir.

GERALD

It's small, he's hiding it.

COLLIN

Like you said, it's small.

PILOT MATTHEWS

We need it sir; all baggage must be
claimed and released.

KENYA grabs COLLIN'S bag revealing the word DRUG ADDICTION in bold RED
letters.

COLLIN

Com'on guys, I've had this bag for years.

GERALD

It's gotta go.

COLLIN aggressively moves to the front of the aircraft

COLLIN

You don't think I've tried to toss this bag
before? It taunts me, day and night.

MACY

Please Collin.

COLLIN

You have no idea what its like for me! If I
could throw it off I would.

GERALD

Don't try to get rid of it yourself. We are
here this time, let us help you.

COLLIN slowly releases his small bag. The group seizes to tumble. LIGHTS RISE to full.

PILOT MATTHEWS

Thank-you all for your cooperation.

Pilot Exit.

FLIGHT ATTENDANT

All passengers, please be seated. The
aircraft is now under control. Please enjoy
a restful journey to Heaven.

Calm settles among the group, they hug one another. Lights Fade.

THE END

ALIVE AND REMAIN

Cast: 5 females.

Alive and Remain is the tale of a young high school student who learns the importance of being an effective witness of God's word.

Themes: Vanity, Witnessing, Pride.

Related Scriptures: Acts 1:8, Romans 10:13-14, Mark 15:15-16, Galatians 2.

Performance of "Alive and Remain"
Photographer: Karla Rodriguez

IN DARKNESS—We hear the sound of girls laughing. Lights Rise on the library at St. Mary's Preparatory School for girls, a privet high school in Stamford Connecticut. The victorian inspired room has wall-to-wall BOOKCASES with an assortment of BOOKS, CANDLES, MINI SCULPTURES and HOUSEPLANTS in ornate pots. Five girls dressed in PREP SCHOOL UNIFORMS sit at a table. The PARTY GIRL and POPULAR GIRL sit stage right, while the WILDCHILD and the FOLLOWER sit stage left. They listen to iPods, read MAGAZINES and paint their nails. BRANDY, a God-fearing Christian girl sits in the center, she is reading her BIBLE.

PARTY GIRL

Honestly, does anyone know the point of study hall? What do teachers expect us to do while we are here?

Girls respond by shaking their head "I don't know"

POPULAR GIRL

Keep your voice down before that mean librarian gives us detention.

WILDCHILD

Who is down for the Gama Frat party Saturday?

PARTY GIRL

I'm going.

POPULAR GIRL

We all need to be there. It will be absolutely amazing.

FOLLOWER

But it's a college party, we could get into so much trouble.

WILDCHILD

And? You afraid of a little slap on the wrist? So what, if we get caught; we get grounded for a few weeks. Big deal.

FOLLOWER

But-

PARTY GIRL

(to Follower)

We are teenagers, these are the years
when we are supposed to get in trouble.

WILDCHILD

We have our whole lives to "follow the
rules".

FOLLOWER

College boys are so intimidating.

WILDCHILD

(eagerly)

I know, don't you just love it?

FOLLOWER

Not really. What about you Brandy, are
you going to the frat party?

The other girls laugh.

BRANDY

It's not my kind of party.

POPULAR GIRL

Yeah, they won't be serving any
communion wine Saturday night.

WILDCHILD

We all know that Brandy is saved and
sanctified.

The other girls mock with shouts of "Hallelujah".

                    BRANDY

                    (boldly)

You need to watch what you say, the Lord
is not mocked.

                    FOLLOWER

Just leave her alone.

                    BRANDY

Yes, please do. Every study hall, you guys
crack jokes on me. All for what? Yeah, I
am a church girl, and I am proud to be
one. Just let me read my bible in peace.
Don't say anything to me, I won't say
anything to you.

                    PARTY GIRL

We were just teasing you Brandy. Man,
church folks are so serious. They can
never take a joke.

                    BRANDY

Not when it's about my Lord and Savior.

                    WILDCHILD

Tell us Brandy, who you taking to the
Prom? John the Baptist?

                    POPULAR GIRL

She doesn't have money for a Prom dress,
spent it all on tithe and offering. Pastor
needs a new Cadillac.

The girls laugh. The CLASS BELL rings. The girls begin to exit.

PARTY GIRL

Just because you stick your nose in a bible
24-7 doesn't mean you better than us.

BRANDY

It means I'm Saved.

PARTY GIRL

Saved from what?

BRANDY

(handing her the bible)

It's all laid out in plain English, read it.

Party Girl gives the bible back then exits.

FOLLOWER

They are just being silly Brandy. They
mean no harm.

BRANDY

Why do you hang out with them?

FOLLOWER

They are cool. I want friends. Don't you?

BRANDY

Jesus is the only friend I need.

FOLLOWER

Oh, okay. If you change your mind about
the party, text me okay?

No response. Follower exits.

BRANDY

(in prayer)

Dear Lord, I have to take this moment
and thank you for saving me from this
world. A world where frat parties, drugs,
sex and alcohol control the minds of my
peers. Where would I be had you not
filled me with your Spirit? I would be lost,
like my classmates. Because of your grace,
I will inherit eternal life. Thank-you,
thank-you Jesus for saving me.

Lights fade to half. Brandy exits then re ENTER with the SOUND of the CLASS BELL.
We then hear the piercing SOUND of a car window SHATTER. Enter a TEACHER,
early 30's, and distraught.

TEACHER

Brandy? There is no study hall today dear.

BRANDY

Study hall is canceled? Why?

TEACHER

You haven't heard.

Silence.

TEACHER

Some of your classmates attended a party
this past Saturday night.

(beat)

There was a terrible car accident.

BRANDY

Is everyone okay?

TEACHER

I'm afraid not.

BRANDY

What hospital? I'll call my Pastor. We can
get some members of my church to go
pray with them.

TEACHER

They're dead Brandy.

(beat)

You should go home. can I call your
parents to come pick you up?

BRANDY

No.

Silence.

BRANDY

Can I just sit here for a moment.

TEACHER

I don't see why not. Will you be okay?

BRANDY

Yes.

Teacher exit. Brandy puts her head down on the table, she is overcome with emotion.

Fade to BLACKOUT with CLASS BELL ringing then the SOUND of the CAR
SHATTER. Lights rise, Party Girl, Popular Girl, Wildchild and Follower are covered
in BLOOD and stand beside Brandy.

PARTY GIRL

Saved from what?

Brandy is startled.

PARTY GIRL

Saved from what? What happens to me
now Brandy? You are the only person I
knew who believed in God. Is it time for
me to go to heaven?

BRANDY

Heaven?

PARTY GIRL

Yes. When people die, that is where they
go right? That is what the bible says right?

BRANDY

I tried to give it to you, but you gave it
back.

PARTY GIRL

I was afraid I wouldn't understand. I tried
to read the bible when I was a little girl,
but needed someone to teach me how to
understand it.

POPULAR GIRL

What does it say about people going to
heaven?

WILDCHILD

It's our time to enter the kingdom of God,
right Brandy.

PARTY GIRL

You are always reading your bible, tell
us how it happens. When do we go to
heaven?

Brandy opens her bible.

BRANDY

"Except a man be born again, he cannot see the kingdom of God." That's what is says here in the book of John.

WILDCHILD

Born again?

BRANDY

It clarifies here "Except a man be born of water and of the Spirit, he cannot enter into the kingdom of God." These words were spoken by Jesus Himself.

POPULAR GIRL

What?

BRANDY

To be born again in water means to be baptized in the name of Jesus. To be born again in spirit means to receive His spirit inside you.

PARTY GIRL

How do we do those things if we are dead?

BRANDY

(beat)

You can't.

The girls panic.

BRANDY

I'm sorry.

POPULAR GIRL

How could you not tell us this? You see
my face everyday. Everyday, you see me,
you knew what I needed to go to heaven,
and you never said one word!

WILDCHILD

No, It can't be. I was a good person. I
never stole. I never murdered, I did lots of
charity work at Christmas. What does the
bible say about that?

Silence

PARTY GIRL

Tell us.

BRANDY

I'm sorry.

PARTY GIRL

Open the bible. Tell us.

BRANDY

Galatians chapter 2,

"We might be justified by faith in Christ
and not by the works of the law; for
by works of the law no flesh shall be
justified."

The others are weeping.

POPULAR GIRL

So, if we can't go to heaven, then we go to-

WILDCHILD

No. Don't say it. Who is Brandy? She is not God. God is the only one who can judge.

PARTY GIRL

Is that right Brandy?

BRANDY

Yes.

(beat)

But we are told in the book of Revelation, God will judge us according to the books.

PARTY GIRL

(Pointing to Brandy's bible)

Those books?

BRANDY

Yes.

WILDCHILD

You knew. You boasted about being "saved" from hell, but you didn't care if I ended up there.

BRANDY

I cared. Honest I did.

POPULAR GIRL

Then how could you let us live our lives and never once invite us to your church?

PARTY GIRL

You shoved a bible in my face, and told
me to read it, I didn't know how.

BRANDY

I'm sorry.

WILDCHILD

You are not. You are alive, you remain
here, you get to go to heaven someday
and we have to go to hell.

PARTY GIRL

Why didn't you tell me?

POPULAR GIRL

Why didn't you tell me?

WILDCHILD

Why didn't you tell me?

BRANDY

Because you were so mean to me! Because
you did bad things.

(beat)

Because I thought being saved made me
better than you. (beat) Because I thought
I had more time.

The girls all exit, with the exception of FOLLOWER.

FOLLOWER

What about me Brandy? I was never
mean to you. I was lonely, I needed Jesus,
but didn't know how to ask for Him. Why
do I have to go to hell?

BRANDY

Because of me.

Blackout. The SOUND of a class bell rings. Bandy covers her head and begins to cry on the table. ENTER PARTY GIRL and POPULAR GIRL who sit stage right, while the WILDCHILD and the FOLLOWER sit stage left. They listen to iPods, read MAGAZINES and paint their nails.

PARTY GIRL

Honestly, does anyone know the point of study hall? What do teachers expect us to do while we are here?

others responds by shaking their head "I don't know"

POPULAR GIRL

Keep your voice down before the evil librarian gives us detention.

WILDCHILD

Who is down for the Gama Fart party Saturday?

BRANDY

No. None of us are. In fact, who ever goes, I will tell your parents.

PARTY GIRL

What?

POPULAR GIRL

Not only are you a creepy church girl, but you a snitch too?

BRANDY

Honestly guys, you go to those parties, get high, get drunk, and then what? Later when you come to, you feel the same desperate feeling for fun you felt before.

Silence.

BRANDY

I got something that will never have you
feeling empty

(to FOLLOWER)

Never have you feeling lonely.

WILDCHILD

Brandy, are you dealing drugs?

BRANDY

No, I'm dealing Jesus. Let me share
something with you I read in my bible
today. Crack jokes if you want to, just
please, give me a chance.

The girls gather closer to Brandy and her open bible. Lights fade.

THE END.

ONE LOST TOO MANY

Cast: 1 female, other 5 characters can be male or female.

One Lost, Too Many was inspired by the 2011 theme for the Sheaves For Christ ministry of the United Pentecostal Church International. The play tells the story of a youth group rescuing a friend from her trials and temptations.

Themes: The Armor of God, Backsliding, Outreach.

Related Scriptures: 2nd Timothy 4:1-5, Ephesians 6.

"One Lost, Too Many" UPCI North American Youth Congress 2011
Photographer David A. Bertram
See live footage of this sketch at www.youtube.com/writeouswordentertainment

Lights Rise—We are in the midst of worship and song service at True Faith Church. SIX CHAIRS sit side-by-side, standing above them are FIVE YOUTH group members. Down stage right is TASHA, late teens. She is blindfolded, her feet and hands are bound and her mouth is covered with DUCK TAPE. The words "JUDGED", "BULLIED", "CURIOSITY", "BODY IMAGE" and "IGNORANCE" are written on cardboard and strung around her neck. She is held hostage by TWO face-less DEMONS with oversized BLACK WINGS. The group collectively SINGS the final words to a praise and worship song. YOUTH MEMBER 1 begins to pass the OFFERING PLATE. The PLATE then passes to YOUTH MEMBER 2. Money is placed inside, and then passed to YOUTH MEMBER 3, then on to YOUTH MEMBER 4. After YOUTH MEMBER 5 places money in the offering plate, the plate is passed to the empty sixth seat. Nobody is there to accept the plate, it falls to the ground.

> YOUTH MEMBER 1
>
> Hey, what's the big idea? That money belongs to the Lord.
>
> YOUTH MEMBER 5
>
> (picking up the money)
>
> I'm sorry. I'm so used to Tasha sitting next to me. She always grabs the plate after me.
>
> YOUTH MEMBER 2
>
> Tasha hasn't been to church in months.
>
> YOUTH MEMBER 3
>
> Yeah, you should be used to her not being here by now.
>
> YOUTH MEMBER 4
>
> Church just isn't the same without her.
>
> YOUTH MEMBER 5
>
> It feels like our youth group has a missing link.

YOUTH MEMBER 1

No way, we are linked by the grace
of God, we can't let Tasha's absence
distract us.

YOUTH MEMBER 3

But it's so hard. We love her. She is our
friend.

YOUTH MEMBER 1

She was our friend. She turned her back
on God, what profitable relationship can
we have with her now?

YOUTH MEMBER 2

But she is lost.

YOUTH MEMBER 1

By her own will.

YOUTH MEMBER 5

But what about God's will? I know He
loves Tasha, the same way He loves me. I
want to give her a call, invite out for ice
cream.

YOUTH MEMBER 1

Are you crazy? Tasha is lost, gone,
backslidden in the world. We must stay
away from her, she might suck us into her
world of sin.

YOUTH MEMBER 2

Maybe we should just let her go through
her trail alone. Let's just have faith Jesus
will bring her back to church.

YOUTH MEMBER 2

Just have faith? Aren't we taught to put our faith to work?

YOUTH MEMBER 5

Amen.

YOUTH MEMBER 1

Just think about all the people in the world, who have never been to church, never opened a bible, never had the chance to feel the sweet presence of Jesus. That is where our focus should be. Tasha knows the word. She was practically born on a church pew. She decided to leave church, that is her problem, not ours.

YOUTH MEMBER 4

I just; wish I knew what she was going through, how she felt.

YOUTH MEMBER 1

We take open prayer request every Sunday morning. She could have said she was struggling.

YOUTH MEMBER 5

(to member 1)

You're being insensitive.

YOUTH MEMBER 3

Tasha is more than some girl who used to sing in choir.

YOUTH MEMBER 2

Or be in my Sunday school class.

YOUTH MEMBER 5

Or sit next to me in church.

YOUTH MEMBER 4

Tasha is a child of God. I'm sorry, but before I go out knocking doors, or run off to the missions field, I have to make sure the people I know here and now have the truth and the peace of the Gospel.

YOUTH MEMBER 1

Tasha knows the truth, she chooses to be lost.

YOUTH MEMBER 2

One lost is too many.

YOUTH MEMBER 5

(to member 1)

I want you guys to hear something I read last night in my bible.

(opens bible)

Here the book Galatians. Chapter

Six. (reading)

"Brethren, if a man be overtaken in a fault, ye which are spiritual, restore such an one in the spirit of meekness; considering thyself, lest thou also be tempted "Bear ye one another's burdens, and so fulfill the law of Christ."

YOUTH MEMBER 2

Tasha is our sister in Christ.

YOUTH MEMBER 3

We should build her up, not tear her
down.

YOUTH MEMBER 1

Alright. What's the plan?

YOUTH MEMBER 5

What are we taught in Ephesians six?

YOUTH MEMBER 2

To put on the whole armor of God.

YOUTH MEMBER 2

The whole armor of God will allow us to
stand against the world and wickedness.

YOUTH MEMBER 5

Exactly.

YOUTH MEMBER 4

Tasha must be without her full armor.

YOUTH MEMBER 5

So we are taking it to her!

YOUTH MEMBER 1

What?

Member 5 removes a large garbage bag from under the seats inside are six pieces of
WAR ARMOR to distribute.

YOUTH MEMBER 5

(to member 2)

You take her helmet of salvation and
breastplate of righteousness.

(to member 3)

You take her shield of faith.

(to member 4)

You will give her, the belt of truth. I will
shod her feet with the Gospel.

(to member 1)

You will give her the sword of the spirit.

YOUTH MEMBER 1

I don't know about this guys.

YOUTH MEMBER 4

That's our sister out there. We have to
allow God, to use us as instruments to
save her.

Lights FLASH. Thrilling Action MUSIC is played. The DEMONS drag Tasha center
stage. The YOUTH MEMBERS each kneel in a stage corner. The Demons can sense
the presence of God near. In animalistic movements, they react.

YOUTH MEMBER 2

I see her.

YOUTH MEMBER 5

Go for it!

YOUTH MEMBER 2

I'm scared. She looks so different, what if
she won't take it.

YOUTH MEMBER 4

Have faith!

YOUTH MEMBER 2 darts out center stage. DEMONS grasp the arms of Youth member 2. they fight off the Demons with the breastplate. The Demons are down, in that moment Youth Member 2 REMOVES the sign "JUDGED" from Tasha's neck. The member demolishes the sign with their feet then places the helmet on Tasha's head and the breastplate around her. TASHA removes her blindfold. As the Demons come to, Youth Member 2 runs away. Other YOUTH MEMBERS cheer and rejoice.

YOUTH MEMBER 5

Who's next?

YOUTH MEMBER 3

I am.

YOUTH MEMBER 3 darts out center stage. DEMONS grasp the arms of Youth Member 3. They WHIP the Demons with the BELT. The Demons are down, in that moment Youth Member 3 REMOVES the sign "CURIOSITY" from Tasha's neck. The member demolishes the sign with their feet then places the shield in her hand. TASHA removes her FOOT ROPES. As the Demons come to, Youth Member 3 runs away. Other YOUTH MEMBERS cheer and rejoice.

YOUTH MEMBER 4

(calling out, while charging center stage)

Jesus, I claim victory for Tasha NOW!

DEMONS grasp the arms of Youth Member 4. they fight off the Demons with the shield. The Demons are down, in that moment Youth Member 4 REMOVES the sign "BODY IMAGE" from Tasha's neck. The member demolishes the sign with their feet then places the shield in her hand. TASHA removes her HAND ROPES. As the Demons come to, Youth Member 4 runs away. Other YOUTH MEMBERS cheer and rejoice.

YOUTH MEMBER 5

(SCREAMING)

IN JESUS NAME—

DEMONS charge toward Youth Member 5. Just as they near, Youth Member 5 dives to the ground sliding to "home-base" which is Tasha's feet. The Demons collide with each other. The Demons are down, in that moment Youth Member 5 REMOVES the sign "IGNORANCE" from Tasha's neck. The member demolishes the sign with their feet then places the shield in her hand. TASHA removes her TAPE from her mouth. As the Demons come to, Youth Member 4 runs away. Other YOUTH MEMBERS cheer and rejoice.

The Demons grab hold of Tasha, she is not yet able to be free.

TASHA

Help me, Jesus, help me! Save me Lord.
Forgive me Jesus. I need you.

YOUTH MEMBER 5

(to member 1)

It's your turn.

YOUTH MEMBER 1

I'm scared! What If I don't make it back?

YOUTH MEMBER 2

Go forward with boldness.

YOUTH MEMBER 5

She needs her full armor! Don't let
someone be lost, because you afraid to
help them find Christ.

YOUTH MEMBER 1 charges toward center stage. DEMONS grasp the arms of Youth Member 1. The Demons CAPTURE Youth Member 1, and begin to place the words around his neck. The SWORD falls to the ground.

YOUTH MEMBER 1

No! No! Help Me! Help Me! Please
Someone Help Me!

TASHA picks up the sword and begins PIERCING the Demons on every side. The Demons are down, Youth Member 1 runs away. Other YOUTH MEMBERS cheer and rejoice. All gather around TASHA who is rejoicing and praising Jesus. She is renewed in Christ. Lights Fade as the group embraces one another.

THE END

THE GOSPEL ACCORDING TO ME

Cast: 2 males, 3 females, 1 Youth Pastor male or female.

The Gospel According To Me is a comedic look at accountability to ministry and evangelism.

Themes: Outreach/Evangelism, Vanity, Humility

Related Scripture: Hebrews 6:10-12

Performance of "The Gospel According to Me"
Photographer: Karla Rodriguez

Lights rise revealing an altar call. Young people are assembled together praying. Emotions flow while hands wave in the air and people cry out in praise and worship. CORWIN: a confident choir director, MEL: a dedicated over achiever, LISA: a somewhat "Stepford Wife" meek girl, ROGER: an innovative wild child of sorts and DEZZY: a passionate soul winner, ALL PRAY with extreme intensity. Up stage center, above all the young people stands the YOUTH PASTOR, who is also praying.

YOUTH PASTOR

(Deeply moved by God's presence)

Our service has come to an end. I want
to encourage those of you praying to
continue to do so. We are surly in the
presence of our Lord Jesus. Seek His
thrown. However, those of you that have
to go, you are dismissed in Jesus name.

Immediately all of the youth spring up from their knees, retrieving to personal conversations, iPod's and CELL PHONES. DEZZY, the exception, continues to pray.

ROGER, engaged in a phone conversation let's out a loud LAUGH.

YOUTH PASTOR

Would you guys mind keeping it down?
We still have people praying in the altar.

ROGER

I am sorry Youth Pastor. (To the group)

Hey, guys zip it!

ROGER kneels close to DEZZY, he watches her pray.

ROGER

Show off.

CORWIN

Roger, what are you doing? She is praying
leave her be.

ROGER

She's just trying to look more spiritual
than the rest of us. The ol' "praying longer
than everyone else trick". I invented it.

CORWIN

I don't know man, she looks pretty
authentic.

ROGER

Yeah, you're right. She probably
committed some big awful sin, and now
she's seeking forgiveness.

(Calling out to Dezzy)

That's it Dezzy! Get your break through!
Get your break through!

DEZZY rises from her knees, she wipes her eyes and smiles; she has connected with
God. She gathers the stack of FLIERS beside her.

YOUTH PASTOR

Dezzy, how are things?

DEZZY

Just great. I have fallen so deeply in love
with Jesus all I want to do is please Him.
There is such a calm in my life these
days. It's the weirdest thing, I have some
problems going on at home and at school,
but I still feel at peace.

YOUTH PASTOR

The peace of God, which passes ALL
understanding is guarding your heart.

DEZZY

Philippians 4:7.

YOUTH PASTOR

Very good.

DEZZY

Ever since I started really studying the
Word, breaking it down, memorizing
it, I've become so powerful and really
excited about sharing it with others.
I want to go door knocking in the
neighborhood. I want to let the people
who live on this block know that our
church is here for them, that Jesus is here
for them.

YOUTH PASTOR

Beautiful. Are these your fliers?

DEZZY

Yes. They have our address and service
times on them.

YOUTH PASTOR

Great. See if you can get some of the
other youth to join you.

(beat)

Dezzy, you feel that fire that is burning in
your heart right now for all of God's lost
children?

DEZZY

Yes.

YOUTH PASTOR

Don't let it blow out.

He exits.

DEZZY

Hey Mel.

MEL

Oh, hi Dezzy, what's been up?

DEZZY

I'm going into the neighborhood to knock
doors and invite people to church. I could
really use your help.

MEL

That's not really my thing Dezzy. Besides
I'm swamped with a bunch of stuff I have
to do. Important stuff.

DEZZY

More important than helping lost souls
find a relationship with Christ? It will
only take a about 45 minutes.

MEL

Don't try to pull a guilt trip on me.
Jesus and I are tight. I know where I'm
supposed to be in my walk with Him.
God did not call me to be a door knocker
or bible study teacher. He called me to be
an Archeological Chemist of Nutrition in
Marine Biology and Technology.

(beat)

The bible say's "to everything there is a
chapter . . ."

DEZZY

Season.

                                MEL

Whatever. This happens to be my chapter.

                                DEZZY

Season.

                                MEL

To reap a good education.

                                DEZZY

The Bible SAYS we are to "Go ye into all
the world, and preach the gospel to every
creature."

                                MEL

First of all, who ever said that wasn't
talking to me because I wasn't there.
Second, I am taking 32 credits this
semester and I have an internship! I have
to go home and study.

Mel puts an IPOD in her ear.

                                CORWIN

Praise the Lord Dezzy. Awesome service
tonight huh?

                                DEZZY

Amazing! I was so moved, God pressed
upon my heart to go invite people in the
community to church.

                                CORWIN

GLORY! Sister, we are in the end time.

                                DEZZY

Amen.

CORWIN

We have to minister to our lost brothers and sisters . . . not today, but right now!

DEZZY

Amen!

CORWIN

(cliché preacher voice)

Let the Lord use you. See you later.

DEZZY

Wait, Brother Corwin, will you join me?

CORWIN

Join you? But I'm the (singing) *Choir Director.*

DEZZY

Yes, I know.

CORWIN

So . . . . I'm the (singing) *Choir Director.* Witnessing, is a job for the Outreach Department.

DEZZY

Isn't all ministry outreach?

CORWIN

No.

DEZZY

But the bible says-

CORWIN

I am not talking about the Bible. I am talking about order of departments! You are trying to mix me up in some other ministry, you're sowing discord amongst the brethren.

DEZZY

I think you are using that scripture out of context.

CORWIN

Hey, I may not read the bible, but I know how and when to use scripture.

DEZZY

Is that right? Well then, teach me a scripture.

CORWIN

(singing)

"*They that wait, upon the Lord—Shall renew in strength—they shall mount up with wings as eagles*". That is scripture, from the book of (he doesn't know)

DEZZY

Isaiah.

CORWIN

Right.

(beat to sing)

"*Cast me not away from thy presence; don't take your spirit from me-*". That is scripture, from the book of Habakkuk.

DEZZY

Psalms.

CORWIN

Yes, well Psalms is the book after
Habakkuk.

DEZZY

No it's not.

CORWIN

The point is Dezzy, I *Sing.* That is my gift.
You do not sing, that is why outreach is
your gift.

DEZZY

But the bible says-

CORWIN

Shhh. I must save my voice. I have choir
rehearsal.

DEZZY

Tonight?

CORWIN

No. Next week Tuesday.

Corwin sits at the KEY BOARD. Dezzy turns to LISA, who sits on a pew gluing
artificial FLOWERS to a HEADBAND.

DEZZY

Hi Lisa.

LISA

Praise the Lord Dezzy.

DEZZY

Do you have 45 minuets to go door knocking with me?

LISA

Oh Dezzy I'm sorry, I cant.

DEZZY

Why not?

LISA

It wouldn't be good for my image.

DEZZY

I'm confused.

LISA

Well, word around church is that Bishop's grandson is coming home from Bible College, and he will need a wife. I am a runner up.

DEZZY

So, if you are trying to become a minister's wife, witnessing will be a great skill to have.

LISA

What for? Minister's wives do not do that kind of stuff. They sing solos, they make hair clips, and they wear neutral colored dresses with matching jackets.

DEZZY

Where exactly in the bible dose it say that ministers wives are exempt from teaching the gospel?

LISA

How am I supposed to know?

(beat)

Would you like to buy a hair clip?

DEZZY

No thanks.

ROGER approaches Dezzy.

ROGER

(Sympathetically)

Hey Dezzy, how's it going?

DEZZY

Good.

ROGER

Yeah? I saw you down at the altar
struggling in spiritual warfare.

DEZZY

Huh?

ROGER

Can I give you a bit of advice? "Let go and
Let God".

DEZZY

Sure thing Roger. Listen, I was wondering
if you would like to go hand out some
tracks with me? Pass out some fliers
about our church to the neighborhood.

ROGER

Dezzy, I would never repeat this to Pastor
or anybody . . . just between you and me,
I am completely opposed to door to door
witnessing.

DEZZY

What? Why?

ROGER

It's dangerous! What if we knock on some
psychopathic person's door and he holds
us hostage.

DEZZY

We are going to stay in the neighborhood,
near familiar faces.

ROGER

Familiar faces? Look, if the person does
not come to our church, then I do not
know them, I don't talk to them, I've got
no time for them. It's a crazy world out
there.

DEZZY

How can you feel so strongly against
something the bible wants us to do?

ROGER

We do not have to go out and witness to
people, God will bring people to us . . .

Dezzy grabs the BIBLE from Roger's hand.

DEZZY

Look there, in the book of Acts,

"And every day, in the temple and from house to house, they kept right on teaching and preaching Jesus as the Christ."

ROGER

Acts, this the Old Testament right?

DEZZY

No.

ROGER

Well, either way, this scripture was written a long, long, long time ago. If you feel pressed to go door knocking, go right ahead . . . like the bible says "If God *behind* you, then who can be against you?"

DEZZY

The bible says-

ROGER

What are you? A bible quizzing gold medalist or something? Chill out.

Roger returns to his conversation.

DEZZY

(to herself)

Chill out? Chill out? How can I chill out when there is a world out side our church doors, lonely, hurt, and discouraged? Looking for something to fill that empty void in their hearts. How can I chill when I know the answer to their longing is with Christ? How can I chill knowing people I see everyday, face an eternity of endless pain when they don't have to? I

cannot "chill". I will not "chill". If only
the people who sit beside me would open
up and their bible, rather than mis-quote
our Pastor. Lord, so many of my friends
have found comfort in their ignorance,
thinking they know so much about a
book they never read.

(beat)

But, I am accountable for me. And I have
a crazy love for your calling.

(beat)

Lord if you have to use me alone to win
every lost soul on this block. Use me.

Dezzy exits the church; LIGHTS slowly FADE on her youth group, whom she has left
behind.

THE END.

COMPANION OF FOOLS

Themes: Modesty, Peer Pressure, Violence, Drug Abuse, Teen Pregnancy,

Related Scriptures: 1st Peter 3:15, Proverbs 13:20, James 4:4

Performance of "Companion of Fools"
Photographer: Karla Rodriguez
Graphic Rite Track Design

The early Disciples of Christ endured unspeakable persecution for the sake of righteousness but still they had hope and apparently, it was obvious to those around them. Peter admonished them to be able to explain to others the reason for their hope in a respectful way. In the wake of tragic incidents, such as school shootings, teen pregnancy, drug abuse and bully-triggered suicides the urgency for young Christians to rise above the influence and be separate from the world is imperative. This is the tale of Saints who rise, and Saints who fall.

Directors Note: The roles of the divas, cheerleaders and activist are all portrayed by the same two female actors. The roles of the mega brothers, jocks, and thugs are all portrayed by the same two male actors.

Cast: 4 females, 4 males.

Darkness. A quick shaft of light spatters center stage. Reveal TONYA'S face. She whispers softly

TONYA

I looked in the mirror today. The
reflection glaring back at me is
unfamiliar. Who am I?

Lights rise. Three middle school students dressed in all BLACK graduation CAP and GOWN stand in a school hallway. TONYA, a vivacious over achiever; NOEL, confident and full of energy; and CAMERON, kind and simple. They are encircled by rusted LOCKERS, loose leaf paper coats the hallway floor. They smile and make awkward poses as if a mob of people are taking their picture.

TONYA

(calling out to audience)

Please mom! Just a few more. My face
hurts.

NOEL

Chill girl, I like it. I feel like a celebrity.

(calling out)

You want some of me by myself dad?

69

CAMERON

C'mon Noel. Let's just finish up, you
know your mom is treating us to brunch.

NOEL

I hope it's some place fancy, like Denny's.

CAMERON

Me too.

TONYA

Can you guys believe it? We are officially
high school freshmen now. I'm so excited!
It's gonna be just like High School
Musical!

NOEL

High school can't come fast enough, four
years to go. Then I get to go live with my
uncle, in Africa.

CAMERON

Oh, the missionary.

NOEL

Yup. My dad says i'm gonna be the
successor of his church. So while you
two love birds are off painting your white
picket fence, I'ma be in AFRICA! A
world famous preacher. I'ma be so cool,
probably wont even have a car, I'll just
ride on a lion up to my church.

TONYA

(shyly)

Be quiet Noel.

NOEL

Don't act shy Tonya. Everybody in church can't wait for yawl to be legal, so yawl can get married.

CAMERON

I'm going to college after high school.

TONYA

Some people get married in college.

CAMERON

Yeah. Your mom mentions that from time to time.

TONYA

My mom says Cameron's gonna be a preacher too. We are getting married. We gonna build a church. Our congregation will be twice as big as yours will.

NOEL

Do you really think some cardboard box church you guys build in Brooklyn will be bigger than my African empire? Please.

TONYA

You think just because you're pastor's son you suppose to have this fancy life.

NOEL

I am.

CAMERON

Guys stop. God's gonna give us all a great life. Let's just worry about high school for right now.

NOEL

Forget that, lets worry about that free
Grand Slam Breakfast right now. C'mon,
we can wait for my parents in the car.

Lights Fade.

The SOUND of a class bell rings, as lights rise, CAMERON sits eating from a LUNCH
TRAY at a CAFETERIA TABLE. Noel enters with a LUNCH TRAY.

CAMERON

There you are. You seen Tonya?

NOEL

Nah. This day been crazy man.

CAMERON

Tell me about it. I didn't know freshmen
get pre college courses!

NOEL

Junior and senior year they make us take
real college classes.

CAMERON

Well, less to take in college.

NOEL

That's the thing, i'm not going to college,
so it's all basically a waist.

CAMERON

There is always the tutoring they offered
at orientation.

NOEL

Who has time for that? Choir practice,
bible quizzing, bible study, I'm swamped.

CAMERON

I'm in the same boat. But, school is only
a few years outta our whole life, it's really
not that bad.

NOEL

I guess.

Tonya enters with her LUNCH.

TONYA

I'm starving.

CAMERON

Having fun? Is it like High School
Musical?

TONYA

Not exactly. But I got an idea; the school
has all these different clubs for students,
but no bible club. Let's start one.

Enter DOREAN, a quiet, withdrawn student sits at the table with her lunch. She goes
unnoticed.

CAMERON

It's not that easy Tonya.

NOEL

Public schools aren't in to religion.

TONYA

I'm not talking about religion, I'm talking about spirituality.

NOEL

Yeah, we know that. But schools are real strict

TONYA

It won't hurt to try.

CAMERON

We could try. What do we have to do?

TONYA

There is a club rally in the gym after school. All we gotta do is get ten people to sign up and be willing to meet at least once a week, and we can be an official club.

NOEL

All Abraham had to do was find ten God loving people to save Sodom and Gomorrah from being destroyed . . . he didn't stand a chance.

TONYA

Well we do stand a chance.

CAMERON

It won't hurt to try Noel. Your dad is always telling us to "go out to the world . . . preach the word".

NOEL

And I plan on doing that. In Africa.

TONYA

So let me get this straight. You can go
all the way to Africa, and pastor over an
empire

NOEL

Empire baby!

TONYA

But you can't muscle up enough strength
to tell ten people in this little bitty school
about Jesus?

NOEL

First of all, Cameron, tell ya girl to stop
worrying abut my muscles and strength,
secondly Tonya, I can get twenty people
to sign up for a bible club.

TONYA

Bet.

NOEL

Bet.

They Exit. Dorean sits alone. Lights Fade.

In Darkness we hear the SOUND of the MEGA PHI MEGA brothers "stepping".
Lights rise revealing two males, in logo t-shirts, well groomed and aggressive. Tonya,
Cameron and Noel watch as the boys perform.

MEGA BROTHER 1

Yehooooo!

MEGA BROTHER 2

Yehooooo!

MEGA BROTHER 1

Fellas! Preeeety Ladies, it's a new year for
the Mega Phi Mega brothers.

MEGA BROTHER 2

A collaborative high school fraternity
that prepares young brothers for the real
college experience.

MEGA BROTHER 1

We are looking for dedicated

MEGA BROTHER 2

Aggressive

MEGA BROTHER 1

Charismatic

MEGA BROTHER 2

Male students, who have a way with
the ladies . . . . and like to have fun. Try
outs for the frat step team are Saturday
morning. Join the brotherhood. Yehoooo!

MEGA BROTHER 1

Yehoooo!

Exit.

Enter the Raging Rockwilder Cheerleading Squad. Two chirpy girls in knee length
cheer outfits and POMPOMS. They are valley-girl personalities

CHEERLEADER 1

Rcokwilders can you hear me?

CHEERLEADER 2

Oh yeah! Oh Yeah!

They growl then scream

                    CHEERLEADER 1

Attention ladies! If you're energetic

                    CHEERLEADER 2

Athletic

                    CHEERLEADER 1

And looking to be apart of a team

                    CHEERLEADER 2

A family

                    CHEERLEADER 1

Then you need to join the Raging
Rockwilder cheer squad. It's fun. Fun.
Fun.

They scream.

                    CHEERLEADER 2

Tryouts are tomorrow at 3pm on the
track field. Come one come all, there is no
place like a cheer squad.

They growl then scream.

                    CHEERLEADER 2

Let's hear it for our championship
winning team!

Enter the Basketball players, two vigorous males in sweats and b-ball jerseys. They have
a jock-like surfer dude personality.

                    PLAYER 1

You may ask yourself why are the
Rcokwilders so great?

PLAYER 2

Why are we so mighty?

PLAYER 1

Where do we get our strength?

PLAYER 2

Our endurance? Its from this right here.

(he points to his heart)

PLAYER 1

We are the gods of the game!

(he holds us a TROPHY in the air)

The cheer squad screams, the players growl.

PLAYER 1

Basketball tryouts this Friday after
school.

All begin to chant "we are the gods of the game" *ala "we are the champions . . ."* as they
Exit. Tonya hesitantly takes the platform.

TONYA

It's funny that you mention God . . . .

CAMERON

We actually are the new bible club.

NOEL

Come one, come all. Before the bell rings
meet the King of Kings!

The SOUND of the class bell rings. Lights fade.

The Rockwilder Basket Ball players are practicing they run a simple drill of passing the ball back and forth. Noel enters.

NOEL

Is anybody interested in bible club? Or how about a home bible study?

PLAYER 1

Beat it freshmeat.

NOEL

Hey, I'm a peaceful guy, just trying to be friends.

PLAYER 2

You are disrespecting holy ground. This is where gods of the game play.

NOEL

I hate to break it to you, but this ground isn't Holy because you guys play on it . . . and you guys aren't gods, there is only one God and he's in heaven.

PLAYER 1

(harshly)

You crazy or something freshmeat?

PLAYER 2

Relax. I like him. He's got guts. What's you're name freshmeat?

NOEL

Noel.

PLAYER 2

You play ball?

NOEL

(reluctant)

Who you think taught LaBron?

The players laugh.

PLAYER 1

You funny freshmeat.

PLAYER 2

It's something about you. That's real
positive. Why don't you try out?

NOEL

Really?

PLAYER 1

Yeah. You can keep my seat on the bench
warm.

Noel joins practice. Enter cheer squad, Tonya follows after.

TONYA

(to cheer squad)

Would anyone like to join bible club? We
only meet once a week.

CHEERLEADER 1

We practice everyday. Sorry.

TONYA

It would only be for an hour, would you take a flyer to think about it?

CHEERLEADER 2

No. We have to focus.

TONYA

I'm new to school. I just wanna make a friend.

CHEERLEADER 1

We are only friends with other cheer squad members. Cheering is a serious sport. It takes dedication.

CHEERLEADER 2

There is no time for any other clubs!

TONYA

I'd be willing to compromise.

CHEERLEADER 1

Compromise what?

TONYA

Well, if you guys just try one bible class, I'd be willing to try the cheer squad.

CHEERLEADER 1

Yeah right, like you have the athletic skills.

CHEERLEADER 2

Let's here you growl.

                    TONYA

Grrrr.

                    CHEERLEADER 2

Growl like a Rockwilder!

                    TONYA

GRAWRRRRRR!

                    CHEERLEADER 1

Great! You can be our mascot. Go suite
up in the locker room.

                    TONYA

Mascot? No way.

                    CHEERLEADER 1

Excuse us? You said you would
compromise.

                    TONYA

But-

                    CHEERLEADER 2

The leader of bible club isn't a liar is she?
That would be a bit contradicting.

                    TONYA

Okay. I'll mascot, but just for a little
while. When are you guys coming to
bible club?

                    CHEERLEADER 1

After the season is over.

Lights fade.

Enter Cameron, passing out flyers to bible club. Noel soon follows wearing the basket ball JERSEY and Tonya wearing a DOG MASCOT costume. DOREAN passes slowly. She is unnoticed by the others.

                    CAMERON

You have to be kidding me. You guys have another game?

                    TONYA

Sorry Cameron.

                    CAMERON

You haven't been to one bible club meeting this whole month.

                    NOEL

Being a Rockwilder takes dedication

                    TONYA

And commitment. How many students joined bible club?

                    CAMERON

None.

                    NOEL

Then we not missing much.

                    CAMERON

This bible isn't gonna create it's self. Besides these games cause you to miss church every Sunday.

                    TONYA

After the season, I bet the whole team will join bible club. We are making so many friends. We can't quit.

Enter players.

PLAYER 1

Hey Noel! Awesome game last week!
Ready for another win?

NOEL

You know it.

Enter Cheer Squad.

CHEERLEADER 1

There's our #1 mascot!

TONYA

Hey guys, I'm ready for another win.

CHEERLEADER 2

After the game there's a huge party at
Mike D's house. His parents are out of
town.

CHEERLEADER 1

There's going to be lots of drinks and lots
of ball players.

TONYA

That's not my scene.

CHEERLEADER 1

Sure it is, you are apart of the team, you
are what we are.

CHEERLEADER 2

And we are all about the *partay*.

TONYA

I don't drink.

CHEERLEADER 1

Well, you will try it.

TONYA

We are not even old enough.

CHEERLEADER 2

That is taken care of.

Scene shifts focus to the players.

PLAYER1

(to Noel)

So you are coming right?

NOEL

Just for a little while.

PLAYER 2

Good. Let's here it everyone!

ALL

(singing)

"We are the gods of the game . . ."

All exit. Lights fade.

Lights rise. Enter Cameron, recruiting for bible club passing out FLYERS to the audience.

CAMERON

(calling out)

Bible club, this Thursday after school.
It's the lamp unto your feet and the light
unto your path!

Enter Noel insistently moving his head to music on an IPOD. He is troubled.

CAMERON

Noel! What's been up, feel like I haven't
seen you in months.

NOEL

Hey.

CAMERON

Is that a new iPod? Let mesee it.

(takes Noel's iPod and he places it
in his ear)

. . . what is this? Since when do you listen
to this stuff?

NOEL

It's just music.

CAMERON

(listening then repeating lyrics)

I'm a real "G" . . . . *I gotta take care of me?
Make my money? Get to the top? Get a
cute chick? Make more than a lot?*

(laughing)

What is this?

NOEL

(annoyed)

It's just music.

CAMERON

Why would you open your mind to words
like this?

NOEL

It motivates me.

CAMERON

To do what? Worry about yourself?
Making it to the top? Dating a cute
girl? He's talking nonsense. A bunch of
materialistic garbage.

(beat)

Why don't you pump this stuff in front of
your dad? If it's just music? Don't front,
listening to it behind close doors . . .

NOEL

What? You judging me?

CAMERON

No, I just feel like your changing. Your
dad always tell us watch what we expose
our minds to, on TV, the internet . . . . it
effects us, we don't realize it, but it does.

NOEL

You are not my pastor!

CAMERON

Right, I'm your friend. This guy motivates
you? How can a person you never even
met motivate you? What are his views on
God?

NOEL

They don't matter.

CAMERON

(disappointed) Wow.

(beat)

Last game of the season huh? It's about three weeks left of school, think your team mates will join bible club?

NOEL

Lay off the whole bible club thing Cameron. All year you've been promoting it, obviously nobody's interested. Besides. They don't talk to me since I missed that shot in the game, cost us the championship.

CAMERON

I heard about that.

NOEL

Everyone has. Its posted all over Facebook and Twitter.

CAMERON

Someone recorded it and posted it on Youtube too!

NOEL

(annoyed)

Cameron.

CAMERON

Sorry man, it will blow over. You pay for
camp yet?

NOEL

I can't go to Church Camp and Basket
Ball Camp.

CAMERON

But I thought you said . . .

NOEL

I gotta get my game back, so I'm better
for next year. I need my team to like me
again, There's this guy on the internet,
his screen name is "dred-dead." He keeps
emailing me, calling me a looser, posting
up all this garbage about me. I can't go
back to being a nobody.

CAMERON

I just learned about that, it's no joke. It's
called cyber-bullying. We can track him
down, we gotta tell a teacher or your
parents.

Enter players, just passing in the hallway.

NOEL

Hey guys what's up?

They ignore him and exit. Noel leaves the opposite way, he is hurt. ENTER Cheer
Squad. Tonya follows dragging her mascot costume.

TONYA

So have you guys thought about it? Can I
be a cheerleader next year?

CHEERLEADER 1

Tonya, we told you. We have the perfect
squad already.

TONYA

Yeah. Well what are you doing this
summer? Can we hang out?

CHEERLEADER 2

How do I say this nicely? NO. We have
cheer camp.

They exit, leaving Tonya behind.

CAMERON

Tonya, wanna go get some ice cream
after school? You have time, now that the
season is over?

TONYA

Sure. Whatever.

She exits. Cameron stands alone. Lights fade.

We hear the SOUND of the class bell. The Mega Phi Mega brothers "step" to center
stage. Noel follows.

MEGA BROTHERS

(chanting)

*Ooh, ah, Mega Phi Mega. Ooh ah Mega
Phi Mega.*

NOEL

What up guys?

MEGA BROTHER 1

Who are you?

NOEL

I'm Noel.

MEGA BROTHER 2

Who's that?

NOEL

Nobody I guess. Can I get down with yawl?

MEGA BROTHER 1

What's your stats?

NOEL

I am a sophomore; I used to play varsity basketball.

MEGA BROTHER 1

Yuck, Jocks.

MEGA BROTHER 2

We don't waist our time running the court with a bunch of sweaty guys. Our free time is invested in the ladies.

NOEL

I dropped them basketball cats a long time ago. They are wack. What is Mega Phi Mega about?

MEGA BROTHER 1

We are a college prep club. Are you going to college?

NOEL

Yeah.

                    MEGA BROTHER 2

Where?

                    NOEL

(thinking)

Probably Harvard or something.

                    MEGA BROTHER 2

(sarcastically)

Right.

                    NOEL

What kind of college prep?

                    MEGA BROTHER 1

We prepare young men for the campus
fraternities, parties, dating-

(to Player 2)

show him that thing you just wrote.

Mega Brother 2 pulls out a PAMPHLET. He hands it to Noel

                    MEGA BROTHER 2

Check this out.

                    NOEL

(reading)

"21 ways to sneak into 21 clubs under the
age of 21". Interesting.

They all exit. Enter DIVA's they have a snobbish personality, and their clothing is fashionably loud, yet stylish. Tonya places her books in her lockers, they notice her.

DIVA 1

Hey prairie.

TONYA

Excuse me?

DIVA 2

You, little house on the prairie.

TONYA

What's that a joke?

DIVA 1

Yes, on you. What's up with you anyway?
Why you always dressed like that? Long
dresses, long hair, you going to churn
butter or something?

DIVA 2

You dress like that cause of your religion
don't you? I knew a girl in middle school
who wore long dresses, long hair, no
jewelry . . . it was cause of her strict
religion.

TONYA

It's just clothing why is it such a problem
for you?

DIVA 1

Cause you think wearing that make you
closer to God.

TONYA

I never said that.

DIVA 1

Where in the bible does it say that
Christian girls have to wear dresses ALL
the time? I'm a Christian and I don't.

DIVA 2

It's what's on the inside that matters.

DIVA 1

Why don't you go back to the leader of
your cult and tell them that everyone
laughs at you because of the way you
dress.

TONYA

(overwhelmed)

My mom makes me dress like this okay!

Silence.

DIVA 1

So forget about your mom, if you wanna
dress cool, wear that stuff out the house,
and when you get to school change your
clothes.

DIVA 2

We should do a makeover!

DIVA 1

You have the potential to be pretty.

DIVA 2

First thing you have to do is loose like
20 pounds. You should do the *Body Like
Beyonce Diet*. It works wonders.

They ALL exit. Enter THUGS, two boys dressed in urban "street" apparel. Noel follows, he is going to his locker. The Thugs stand on opposite sides of the stage, guarding themselves intently.

> THUG 1
>
> (to Noel)
>
> Yo shorty, you looking for some product?

> NOEL
>
> Some what?

> THUG 2
>
> Some "get right"?

> NOEL
>
> Oh, no. I'm cool.

> THUG 1
>
> Yeah you look like a sucka.

> NOEL
>
> I'm no sucka, and I'm tired of being disrespected.

> THUG 2
>
> Yo, calm down Steve Urkel.

> THUG 1
>
> I know you; you roll with those pretty-boy Mega Brothers.

> NOEL
>
> (hesitating)
>
> I drop them cats. They are wack. Yawl go to school here?

THUG 1

Yeah. We class of 2007, we just ain't
graduate yet.

NOEL

I'm Noel.

THUG 2

We *Cell Block 2D*. "D" stands for deep.

THUG 1

We rappers. Check it-

Thug 2 beat-boxes, while Thug 1 raps.

THUG 1

(rapping)

*A 'G' like me never go to class, I take
sucka's like you, make 'em moe my grass.*

THUG 2

We had a record deal, but our manager
got locked up.

THUG 1

Soon as he finishes serving 10 to 15, we
blowin' up!

NOEL

I'm trying to roll with a crew, can I be
down?

THUG 1

This ain't no game young homie. While
we waiting on our record deal, we out

here in these school hallways trying to make that cake.

NOEL

Like birthday cake?

THUG 2

No, fool. This kinda cake.

(*he holds up a stack of CASH*)

THUG 1

You ain't really tryin' to be family.

NOEL

Yes I am. I wanna be family.

THUG 2

It would be cool if we became "Cell Block 3D", then we could walk around with those movie glasses on all the time. We'd look so cool.

THUG 1

Yeah, that would be tight.

(to Noel)

But this is serious stuff. These school hallways are real rough shorty.

THUG 2

I put my life on the line out here every day, I'm tryin' to feed my daughter.

THUG 1

You have a daughter?

THUG 2

No, not really, but rappers say that all the
time, I'm just tryin' to sound authentic.

(pause, he has an idea)

That should be the name of our album . . .
Authentic.

THUG 1

(to Noel)

You can't just be down with us, you gotta
do some gang related violence or you
gotta get shot at and look cool like 50
cent.

NOEL

You guys wanna shoot me?

THUG 1

No, we want you to shoot at somebody.
Initiation.

(he pulls out a GUN and hands it
to Noel)

THUG 2

See that, you said you tired of being
disrespected; this makes you a real man.

The SOUND of the class bell rings. Lights fade.

The silhouette of DOREAN appears in light.

Lights rise on DOREAN. She is motionless.

She is dressed in all BLACK clothing. She appears tiresome, and discouraged.

DOREAN

> (a spoken word poem read from
> her journal, addressing the
> audience.)

> Why do I have to feel all alone on the
> inside? Trapped in my thoughts I just
> wanna die.
> Hurt by the joke you just said.
> Thoughts of taking my life running
> through my head.
> I didn't ask for people to use me.
> I didn't ask for a father who abuses me.
> Sitting here alone, no more tears to cry.
> God if you're out there save me from this
> suicide.

Lights fade.

In Darkness we hear the voice of ACTIVIST 1. She is protesting, Lights rise to reveal her and ACTIVIST 2. Two ultramodern personalities, dressed in avant-garde clothing.

ACTIVIST 1

> Human rights! Human freedom of
> expression for all! Let know government,
> no parent, no religion restrict your
> lifestyle!

> (repeat)

ACTIVIST 2 passes out flyers. DOREAN enters, she wears ALL BLACK. She listens to the rants for a moment, then exits. Tonya enters to her locker. She pulls a short RED MINI SKIRT out her bookbag. Places it around her hips, then heads to put it on. She is interrupted by ACTIVIST 1.

ACTIVIST 1

> (to Tonya)

> Hey, church girl. Guess you're here to
> shut me down?

TONYA

No, I'm just on my way to the bathroom.

ACTIVIST 2

You call the principle on us, and we will
chain ourselves to these lockers.

TONYA

I'm not calling anyone, honest.

ACTIVIST 1

I hope you know it's people of the
Christian faith who are out violently
taking the lives of abortion doctors. Hath
God not said thou shalt not kill?

TONYA

Um . . . . I can't speak for those people. I
can only speak for what I believe.

ACTIVIST 1

It's Christians who lock their church
doors to homosexuals. Hath God not said
to love thy neighbor?

TONYA

Um, At my church we believe in living
a biblical lifestyle, but we never shut the
doors to any child of God.

ACTIVIST 2

I don't believe you. All Christians are the
same. You show me, show me where the
bible says I can't be who I want to be and
still love God. Show me where it says God
is a man and not a woman?

ACTIVIST 1

She can't! Everyone break free of religious
order, be who you want to be!

(to Tonya)

Beat it church girl.

Tonya is overwhelmed with emotion, Cameron enters.

CAMERON

Tonya? Sweetheart what's wrong?

ACTIVIST 1

Well look what the cat dragged in?

CAMERON

Don't start with me.

ACTIVIST 1

Your girlfriend already started it.
Condemning us, judging us . . .

TONYA

I did not, I was minding my own
business.

ACTIVIST 2

We are just trying to express our views.

CAMERON

Fine. But why do you guys stop me every
time I try to express mine?

ACTIVIST 1

Because your's are fictional, brainwashing
and cult-like.

CAMERON

You're entitled to your opinion.

ACTIVIST 1

Why don't you show us? Show us your "word of God" show us your narrow minded views.

CAMERON

I've invited you guys to bible club for the past two years.

ACTIVIST 1

Why cant you do it now? Give us a scripture, just one.

CAMERON

We're leaving.

ACTIVIST 1

Cowards! Give us a scripture, about abortion, about male/female marriage, about drinking alcohol. You can't. Every time I ask a Christian to back their beliefs, they gotta "get back to me" or "go find a bible". If you love the word of God so much how come you don't carry it with you?

CAMERON

My bible's in my bookbag.

ACTIVIST 2

Then give us a scripture.

CAMERON

You want a scripture? Fine. Ephesians 5:6 "Let no man deceive you with vain words" 1Timothy 6:4 "He is proud, knowing nothing, but doting about questions and strifes of words, "2nd Timothy 2:16 "But shun profane and vain babblings: for they will increase unto more ungodliness"1 Timothy 3:16 "And without *controversy* great is the mystery of godliness". You wanna step to me? Fine. But let me warn you, it's not me your up against, it's the word of God. And it's sharper than any two-edged sword, Hebrews 4:12!

(beat)

I would love to open up the bible and show you whatever you want to know. I am not going to argue with you.

Activist 1 leaves flustered.

ACTIVIST 2

(to Cameron)

I'd like that. A chance to talk. No arguing, just talk.

CAMERON

Thursdays, after school.

exit Activist 2.

TONYA

How do you do that? Just blurt out scripture?

CAMERON

I remember some from bible quizzing, but mostly because, I read the bible everyday. Knowing the scriptures make us wise.

TONYA

I can't take much more of this harassment
Cameron.

CAMERON

I know what you mean. I can't stand
being teased either.

TONYA

It's easier for you, people can't tell your
beliefs based on the way you look. I just
want friends, no restrictions. I just wanna
kick back and have fun.

CAMERON

You think we gonna know these people
forever Tonya? We're not.

TONYA

Sometimes I feel like they have a point.
Why do we have to be so different? It's
embarrassing. It makes people not wanna
come to church with us.

CAMERON

If you are embarrassed about who
you are, people can sense it. They will
challenge you.

TONYA

Doesn't the bible say God cares about the
inside?

CAMERON

Yes, in several places. I can think of a
scripture now, in 1st Samuel, "man looks
at the outward appearance, but God looks
at the heart".

TONYA

Exactly!

CAMERON

Not so fast, there are just as many
scriptures that talk about being different
than those who don't love God and those
who don't obey His commandments.

TONYA

I'm not going to Hell just because I stop
dressing like a character form Little
House on the Prairie.

CAMERON

You obviously have your mind made up
that you gonna dress the way YOU want,
so you gonna find every excuse in the
book to justify it. Let's not argue.

TONYA

I wanna have fun.

CAMERON

So do I, I have friends. I'm in clubs like
soccer team, yearbook club, I chill at
the pep rallies, but when stuff starts
compromising God I take a step back.

TONYA

You can't just drop out of clubs.

CAMERON

Why not? Where does our loyalty lie?
With God? Or some click?

TONYA

The bible is constantly contradicting.

CAMERON

Perhaps to the naked eye. Aren't we
told to rightly divide the word of God?
To study to show ourselves approved?
Anybody who just flips open a bible
can be confused, but when you study it,
research, make connections, it all comes
together.

(beat)

Come to bible club, help me teach.

TONYA

Cameron, the only scripture I know by
heart is John 3:16.

CAMERON

That's not true.

TONYA

It is, I quote stuff I hear my mom say . . .
but

(beat)

I gotta go meet some friends.

CAMERON

What about ice cream?

TONYA

Tomorrow.

She exits.

CAMERON

You said that yesterday.

The SOUND of the bell rings. Noel enters in a HOODED JACKET.

CAMERON

Noel, that you?

NOEL

Get a way from me!

CAMERON

Chill out man, I just wanna say hi.

NOEL

Did you here what I said? Let me make myself a bit clearer.

> (he pulls GUN from his bookbag
> and points it toward Cameron)

Get a way from me.

CAMERON

(nervous)

What are you doing? Get that out my face man.

NOEL

You think I'm a sucka? You tryin to disrespect me?

CAMERON

(fearful for his life)

Noel please.

NOEL

I could smoke you right now. You and
half this school. And I wouldn't go out
like them cats in the mid-west, taking
my own life after I'm finish, no, I'd walk
outta this place with my head high, cause
I'm a real "G".

CAMERON

In the name of Christ Jesus I rebuke this
weapon.

NOEL

Say what?

CAMERON

I rebuke it.

NOEL

I will shoot you.

CAMERON

I rebuke it.

Silence.

Noel puts the gun in his waist.

NOEL

You the sucka Cameron.

Noel exits. Lights Fade.

At Rise: A musical interlude plays while actors act out/ mime the following stage
directions.

*Cameron and Tonya walk through a park holding hands. He stops, caresses her cheek.
They laugh.*

He gives her a FLOWER. She hugs him, then she smells the flower. They hold hands and laugh more.

Player 1, Thug 2, Diva 2, Activist 1 enter. They pull Tonya away from Cameron. They pass a bottle of alcohol back and forth, Tonya refuses a few times, but finally drinks.

Tonya walks back to Cameron, she is obviously drunk. He tries to woo her with A DOZEN ROSES, she hardly notices

Player 1, Thug 2, Diva 2, and Activist 1 pull Tonya away from Cameron. They light a LIGHTER and pass "smoke" back and forth, Tonya refuses a few times, but finally smokes.

Tonya walks back to Cameron. He tries to give her a HEART BOX OF CHOCOLATE. She is too wasted to notice.

Player 1, Thug 2, Diva 2, and Activist 1 pull Tonya away from Cameron. They pass smoke, alcohol, and pills back and forth. Tonya indulges, soon the group circles her with their activity. Everyone gathers around Tonya, she is masked from audience Tonya is transforming/changing her appearance.

We see the "new" Tonya. She wears a T-shirt of FLAMES, red lips, fishnet tights, and a skirt knee length, but covered in jewels and chains. Cameron hands her the chocolate heart, before she can grab it she's whisked away by the group. They exit. Leaving Cameron alone.

Lights dim. Re-enter Tonya

CAMERON

What took you so long? I've been waiting
for hours. What are you wearing?

TONYA

Clothes.

CAMERON

What's your shirt mean?

TONYA

I don't know, it was a gift.

CAMERON

I bought you a gift

(handing her the chocolate)

TONYA

I'm on a diet.

CAMERON

Your always on a diet.

(she hands it back)

TONYA

I'm on my way to an after party. I can't
stay long.

CAMERON

I got you something else.

(he hands her a plane ticket)

TONYA

What's this?

CAMERON

A plane ticket. For the missions trip this
summer. We old enough to go now. You
gotta come.

TONYA

I wish you would have told me, before
you spent your money on this. I'm going
to Atlantic City this summer, to hang out
with some friends.

CAMERON

The whole summer?

TONYA

Yeah.

CAMERON

Other guys going?

TONYA

Yeah, who happen to like the way I dress.

Silence.

CAMERON

Maybe we need to take a break Tonya.

TONYA

You can't break up with me!

CAMERON

Because you love me right?

TONYA

Sure I love you, But my mother will kill
me if we break up!

Shocked at her response, Cameron exits.

TONYA

Cameron come back here! Cameron!.

Lights Fade.

The SOUND of the class bell rings. Cameron enters to his locker. Tonya and Mega
Brother 2 cross him arm and arm. They are dating. DOREAN enters. She wears all
black and stands beside him. She wears all black clothing

DOREAN

No more bible club this year?

CAMERON

What? Oh, well you know they say Junior
year is the most important . . . . besides,
nobody ever came.

Silence.

DOREAN

(whispers in sadness)

I'm going to kill myself tomorrow.

CAMERON

Excuse me?

She begins to walk away.

CAMERON

Wait, what did you say?

DOREAN

You heard me.

CAMERON

I forgot your name.

DOREAN

You never knew it.

CAMERON

I'm Cameron.

DOREAN

This isn't some sympathy plea. I'm not trying to go out all dramatic. Leaving a bunch of clues and notes.

(beat)

Something told me to tell you.

CAMERON

Can we talk?

DOREAN

Don't feel sorry for me!

CAMERON

I don't.

DOREAN

I'm not weak.

CAMERON

I know. Weak people give up when it gets too difficult. Wise people ask for help.

Silence.

CAMERON

I wanted to kill myself when my dad left me. But before I did it. God saved me.

DOREAN

I'd of been better off, if my father had just left. Instead of sticking around, and doing the things he did to me.

CAMERON

Can I show you some scriptures, that
helped me learn to get over what my Dad
did to me?

DOREAN

Yes.

A music interlude is played as Cameron and Dorean read the bible. Moments later
ACTIVIST 2, MEGA BROTHER 1, THUG 2, CHEERLEADER 1 enter and Cameron
gives them bibles from his book bag. Cameron mimes teaching gestures as

Lights fade.

Lights rise. Cameron and Dorean sit together reading a bible. Dorean now wears
vibrant clothing.

CAMERON

Do you remember me teaching you about
the book of Acts?

DOREAN

(delighted)

yes.

CAMERON

The Spirit of Christ Jesus living inside of
you is what brings you daily joy.

DOREAN

Learning about Jesus has brought such
peace to my life Cameron.

Dorean, stands with Cameron. They pass out Flyers for bible club. Moments later
Cameron exits off stage, Tonya, Diva 1, and Diva 2 enter.

DIVA 1

Tonya, look there. Grim Reaper is all over
your ex.

TONYA

Grim Reaper?

DIVA 2

You know, that weird girl who use to
wear all black, now she dressing all cute
and hanging all over Cameron.

TONYA

She's not all over him, besides. I dumped
him, so who cares.

DIVA 1

You care! She can't date your ex, he used
to be your man!

DIVA 2

Go ask her if she wanna fight you for
him.

TONYA

No way, I can't fight.

DIVA 1

We got your back. You can't let her
disrespect you like this.

Tonya crosses to Dorean.

TONYA

What up prairie, you going to churn
butter or something?

DOREAN

Would you like to come to bible club?

TONYA

I'd like you to stay away from my man!
Cameron.

DOREAN

We are just friends.

TONYA

Keep it that way.

Dorean smiles in confusion and exits. Enter Noel.

DIVA 1

Hey Tonya, ain't that the dude from Cell
Block 3D?

TONYA

Who Noel? Wow, he looks different.

DIVA 2

Yawl would look cute together.

TONYA

No way, I've known him since we were
kids.

DIVA 1

He's cool any girl would die to be with
him.

TONYA

Really?

DIVA 2

Yes.

(she pushes Tonya toward Noel)

TONYA

Hey Noel.

NOEL

Tonya? Nobody calls me that anymore.
How are you?

TONYA

Good.

NOEL

You look good.

TONYA

You too.

NOEL

Those girls your friends?

TONYA

Yeah.

NOEL

(calling to the Divas)

Hey ladies.

DIVAS

Heyyyy.

NOEL

So what's up? You wanna hang out after
school?

TONYA

I don't know. I feel like we don't even
know each other anymore.

NOEL

C'mon, it's me. Noel. From nursery
school. You know me.

TONYA

My mom doesn't get home till late.

NOEL

Good. We can catch up.

The SOUND of the class bell rings. Lights Fade.

Lights rise. Cameron sits on a park bench, he prays.

CAMERON

Lord, I know it's been some time since
me and Tonya spoke. She's the only girl
I ever loved. Fix her Lord make her into
the sweet girl she was when we were kids.
I want to be with her, forever. But—Let
your will be done.

Enter Tonya.

TONYA

Cameron?

CAMERON

Hey.

TONYA

How you been?

CAMERON

Good. Great. You?

TONYA

Alright.

CAMERON

I brought you this.

He hands her a TUBE of CHIPS

CAMERON

They're fat free Pringles . . . cause your always dieting.

They laugh.

TONYA

Thanks.

CAMERON

I never expected to start senior year to be like this. By now, you were suppose to be planning our wedding.

TONYA

(giggling)

Oh yeah. We use to have a lot of fun.

CAMERON

We can again. If you want to, get back together. I know it's been a long time, but we can try.

Silence.

                              CAMERON

Please. I love you.

                              TONYA

Cameron, I'm pregnant.

                              CAMERON

What?

                              TONYA

I'm so sorry.

                              CAMERON

Sorry! What is wrong with you! What
happened to you?

                              TONYA

        (tearful)

I'm sorry.

                              CAMERON

By that Mega Phi Mega dude?

Silence

                              TONYA

By Noel.

                              CAMERON

No.

                              TONYA

I can fix this.

CAMERON

How?

TONYA

I could do the same thing with you.

CAMERON

What? That is not what I want! How can
that be what you want for yourself? Look
in the mirror Tonya. Have you seen what
you turned into?

Cameron exit.

TONYA

I'm sorry.

Lights fade.

Lights rise. Tonya sits alone eating lunch. Enter Dorean.

DOREAN

You're all alone. Where are your friends?

TONYA

I guess I don't have any. You are-

DOREAN

Dorean.

TONYA

You go to my old church? I can tell you
are a Christian by the way you look.
Church makes you dress like that.

DOREAN

Well, not exactly. Modesty is a standard
at church, so for a while that is why I did.
Which was okay. God honors obedience.
But, after a while, I felt strange, doing
things but not knowing the reasons why

TONYA

Like a puppet.

DOREEN

I got a bible, and I asked women at
church to teach me from the bible about
modesty, then I asked Pastor to teach me
about salvation, and baptism. I learned
WHY. Now, I preach the bible because I
understand it for myself, because it is the
truth. I dress this way, because it is my
witness. When people look at me, I want
them to see something different from the
world. I want them to see God. (beat) will
you ever come to bible club Tonya?

TONYA

I don't know. I have class. See you around.

DOREAN

You should come back to church Tonya.
Regardless of what people might think
or say about you. Regardless of how
embarrassed you may feel. Never let
anything stop you from spending eternity
with Jesus.

Tonya exits. Lights fade.

Lights Rise on Cameron standing at a PODIUM in a CAP and GOWN. He addresses
the audience.

CAMERON

(reading)

Family, Friends, Faculty, Graduates.
I am proud to stand here today as
valedictorian of the class of 2010. We've
had challenges and trials, but we made
it to this point. A place in our lives
where we can look back, and say we
have overcome. There have been lessons
learned, and homework lost. But we've
come this far, not to regret, not to forget,
but to continue. Freshman year, I learned
about a famous poet in English class by
the name of Robert Frost. His famous
poem "The Road Not Taken" sparked an
interest to me. He writes in his final lines,
I quote: "Two roads diverged in a wood,
and I' . . . I took the one less traveled by,
And that has made all the difference." I
always imagined being the traveler who
took the road less traveled by. Then one
day I came across the biblical scripture
Matthew 7:13. It reads:

"Enter ye in at the strait gate: for wide
is the gate, and broad is the way, that
leadeth to destruction, and many there
be which go in thereat: Because strait is
the gate, and narrow is the way, which
leadeth unto life, and few there be that
find it." That's when I realized Robert
Frost had it all wrong. It doesn't matter if
less or more people have traveled down
the road you chose. Either one could be
the road that leads to destruction. My
prayer for my fellow classmates is that
you all chose the narrow road, the narrow
way, it will lead you to a life of eternal
happiness. God Bless you all. Thank you.

Lights fade.

Tonya sits alone with a baby in a stroller. Moments later, Cameron enters with a
SUITCASE.

123

CAMERON

Hey you.

TONYA

(overjoyed)

Hi Cameron.

CAMERON

(peaking at her baby)

She is beautiful.

TONYA

Thank-you. Congratulations on graduation. They announced it at church Sunday. I am getting my GED this fall.

CAMERON

Good, I knew you would be alright. Glad you are back at church. How is Noel?

TONYA

I have not seen him in months. Off to Bible College? To start your cardboard box church in Brooklyn?

CAMERON

Not exactly.

TONYA

I thought you were going to become a preacher?

CAMERON

I preach, minister, evangelize, all of those titles. I talk to people about God everyday. I am going to Michigan State. I am majoring in social work.

CAMERON

TONYA

Really?

CAMERON

Yeah, there are a lot of people out there that grow up with no father in the house, like I did. I want to help them discover the Father within them.

TONYA

I am proud of you. Take care Cameron.

(beat)

Goodbye.

CAMERON

Be seeing you Tonya.

Cameron crosses to exit. He is cut short by Noel, standing on a street corner.

CAMERON

Noel? Is that you?

NOEL

Hey Cameron, what up with you?

CAMERON

Leaving for college.

NOEL

Cool. You looking for some product? Got some stuff that will make you feel good.

Silence

125

NOEL

(embarrassed)

Ah, I'm just kidding with you.

CAMERON

Right.

NOEL

Congratulations on graduating.

CAMERON

Thanks. Take care.

(beat)

I pray for you all the time Noel.

NOEL

Thank-you.

Cameron exits, Noel exits the opposite way. A shaft of light reveals Tonya as she rocks her baby.

TONYA

I looked in the mirror today. The reflection glaring back is becoming clearer. I am a child of God.

Lights fade.

THE END.

Six bible themed scripts with contemporary plotlines for youth ministry.

A drama team has the exciting job of doing what any pastor or evangelist does from a pulpit, however we get to make it sparkle. We add lights, backdrops, funny characters and sound effects. Still, it is important for us to have a clear message and a well-organized story to effectively minister. We need to touch the hearts of our audience. This book is designed for the drama team that is ready to see lives changed through their performance. *Touch Ten Souls in Ten Minutes* is a collection of short contemporary plays full of scripture and entertaining plotlines that emphasize topics such as *Backsliding, Body Image, Bullying, Drug Abuse, Gossip, Music, Modesty, Peer Pressure, Prayer,* and many more. A simple ten-minute play has the power to touch the hearts of ten young souls and change their walk in Christ forever.

Buffalo New York native April Baskin has studied dramatic arts for over ten years. She is a member of The Actors Equity Association and currently serves as a drama coordinator for the New York Metro Youth District of the UPCI and several Christian conferences in the New York City area. April actively spreads the gospel of Christ through filmmaking, theatre and teaching acting as ministry seminars. She currently resides in Brooklyn NYC with her husband and daughter.